JOHN STOTT BIBLE STUDIES

12 Studies with Commentary for Individuals or Groups

Ephesians

Building a Community in Christ

John
STOTT

with Phyllis J. Le Peau

Inter-Varsity Press
Nottingham, England

IVP Connect
An imprint of InterVarsity Press
Downers Grove, Illinois

InterVarsity Press, USA
P.O. Box 1400, Downers Grove, IL 60515-1426, USA
World Wide Web: www.ivpress.com
Email: email@ivpress.com

Inter-Varsity Press, England
Norton Street, Nottingham NG7 3HR, England
Website: www.ivpbooks.com
Email: ivp@ivpbooks.com

InterVarsity Press®, USA, is the book-publishing division of InterVarsity Christian Fellowship/USA®, a student movement active on campus at hundreds of universities, colleges and schools of nursing in the United States of America, and a member movement of the International Fellowship of Evangelical Students. For information about local and regional activities, write Public Relations Dept., InterVarsity Christian Fellowship/USA, 6400 Schroeder Rd., P.O. Box 7895, Madison, WI 53707-7895, or visit the IVCF website at <www.intervarsity.org>.

Inter-Varsity Press, England, is closely linked with the Universities and Colleges Christian Fellowship, a student movement connecting Christian Unions in universities and colleges throughout Great Britain, and a member movement of the International Fellowship of Evangelical Students. Website: www.uccf.org.uk.

All Scripture quotations, unless otherwise indicated, are taken from the Holy Bible, New International Version®. NIV®. Copyright © 1973, 1978, 1984 by International Bible Society. Used by permission of Zondervan Publishing House. Distributed in the U.K. by permission of Hodder and Stoughton Ltd. All rights reserved. "NIV" is a registered trademark of International Bible Society. UK trademark number 1448790.

This study guide is based on and includes excerpts adapted from The Message of Ephesians *©1979 by John R. W. Stott, originally published under the title* God's New Society.

Design: Cindy Kiple
Images: Richard Drury/Getty Images

USA ISBN 978-0-8308-2163-1
UK ISBN 978-1-84474-319-3

Printed in the United States of America ∞

P   23   22   21   20   19   18   17   16   15   14   13   12   11   10

Y   27   26   25   24   23   22   21   20   19   18   17   16   15   14

Introducing Ephesians

One of our chief evangelical blind spots has been to overlook the central importance of the church. We tend to proclaim individual salvation without moving on to the saved community. Our message is more good news of a new life than of a new society.

Nobody can emerge from a careful reading of Paul's letter to the Ephesians with an individual gospel. For Ephesians is the gospel of the church. It sets forth God's eternal purpose to create through Jesus Christ a new society which stands out in bright relief against the somber background of the old world.

This vision of a renewed human community has stirred me deeply. At the same time, the realities of the lovelessness and sin in so many churches are enough to make one weep, for they dishonor Christ. Yet increasing numbers of church members are seeking the church's radical renewal. For the sake of the glory of God and the evangelization of the world, nothing is more important than the church becoming God's new society.

Getting to Know the Ephesians

In verse 1 Paul describes his readers as "saints" because they belong to God; they are "the faithful" or "believers" because they have trusted in Christ; and they have two homes, for they reside equally "in Ephesus" and "in Christ Jesus."

Originally a Greek colony, Ephesus was now the capital of the Roman province of Asia and a busy commercial port. It was also the headquarters of the cult of the goddess Diana (or Artemis) whose temple, after being destroyed in the middle of the fourth century B.C., had gradually been rebuilt to become one of the seven wonders of the world.

A Message for Us
The letter focuses on what God did through the historical work of Jesus Christ and does through his Spirit today, in order to build his new society in the midst of the old. The subjects can be divided as follows:

1. The new life which God has given us in Christ (1:3—2:10)

2. The new society which God has created through Christ (2:11—3:21)

3. The new standards which God expects of his new society, especially unity and purity (4:1—5:21)

4. The new relationships into which God has brought us—harmony in the home and hostility to the devil (5:21—6:24)

The whole letter is thus a magnificent combination of Christian doctrine and Christian duty, Christian faith and Christian life, what God has done through Christ and what we must be and do in consequence.

Suggestions for Individual Study
1. As you begin each study, pray that God will speak to you through his Word.

2. Read the introduction to the study and respond to the question that follows it. This is designed to help you get into the theme of the study.

3. The studies are written in an inductive format designed to help you discover for yourself what Scripture is saying. Each study deals with a particular passage so that you can really delve into the author's meaning in that context. Read and reread the passage to be studied. The questions are written using the language of the New International Version, so you may wish to use that version of the Bible. The New Revised Standard Version is also recommended.

4. Each study includes three types of questions. *Observation* questions ask about the basic facts: who, what, when, where and how.

Interpretation questions delve into the meaning of the passage. *Application* questions (also found in the "Apply" section) help you discover the implications of the text for growing in Christ. These three keys unlock the treasures of Scripture.

Write your answers to the study questions in the spaces provided or in a personal journal. Writing can bring clarity and deeper understanding of yourself and of God's Word.

5. In the studies you will find some commentary notes designed to give help with complex verses by giving further biblical and cultural background and contextual information. The notes in the studies are not designed to answer the questions for you. They are to help you along as you learn to study the Bible for yourself. After you have worked through the questions and notes in the guide, you may want to read the accompanying commentary by John Stott in the Bible Speaks Today series. This will give you more information about the text.

6. Move to the "Apply" section. These questions will help you connect the key biblical themes to your own life. Putting the application into practice is one of the keys to growing in Christ.

7. Use the guidelines in the "Pray" section to focus on God, thanking him for what you have learned and praying about the applications that have come to mind.

Suggestions for Members of a Group Study

1. Come to the study prepared. Follow the suggestions for individual study mentioned above. You will find that careful preparation will greatly enrich your time spent in group discussion.

2. Be willing to participate in the discussion. The leader of your group will not be lecturing. Instead, she or he will be encouraging the members of the group to discuss what they have learned. The leader will be asking the questions that are found in this guide.

3. Stick to the topic being discussed. Your answers should be based on the verses which are the focus of the discussion and not on outside authorities such as commentaries or speakers. These studies focus on a particular passage of Scripture. Only rarely should you refer to other portions of the Bible. This allows for everyone to participate on equal ground and for in-depth study.

4. Be sensitive to the other members of the group. Listen attentively when they describe what they have learned. You may be surprised by their insights! Each question assumes a variety of answers. Many questions do not have "right" answers, particularly questions that aim at meaning or application. Instead the questions push us to explore the passage more thoroughly.

When possible, link what you say to the comments of others. Also, be affirming whenever you can. This will encourage some of the more hesitant members of the group to participate.

5. Be careful not to dominate the discussion. We are sometimes so eager to express our thoughts that we leave too little opportunity for others to respond. By all means participate! But allow others to also.

6. Expect God to teach you through the passage being discussed and through the other members of the group. Pray that you will have an enjoyable and profitable time together, but also that as a result of the study you will find ways that you can take action individually and/or as a group.

7. It will be helpful for groups to follow a few basic guidelines. These guidelines, which you may wish to adapt to your situation, should be read at the beginning of the first session.

☐ Anything said in the group is considered confidential and will not be discussed outside the group unless specific permission is given to do so.

☐ We will provide time for each person present to talk if he or she feels comfortable doing so.

☐ We will talk about ourselves and our own situations, avoiding conversation about other people.

☐ We will listen attentively to each other.

☐ We will be very cautious about giving advice.

8. If you are the group leader, you will find additional suggestions at the back of the guide.

1
A LIFE OF
SPIRITUAL BLESSING

Ephesians 1:1-14

*H*ow quickly we forget what is ours when we become followers of Jesus. Paul delighted in reminding the believers at Ephesus about the spiritual blessings that were theirs because they belonged to Christ. But these blessings were not for them as individuals. Nor are they for us alone. They belong to the church. Our tendency is to proclaim individual salvation without moving on to the saved community. Christ died to "purify for himself a people that are his very own" (Titus 2:14). Ephesians is the gospel of the church and to the church, God's new society.

Open

■ How does being a part of a Christian community help you to see God at work?

Study

1. *Read Ephesians 1:1-10.* What information does the introduction to this book give (vv. 1-2)?

---

2. We are told in verse 3 that we are blessed with "every spiritual blessing in Christ." Carefully list each of the blessings in verses 4-8.

---

3. As you reflect on these blessings, what contributions do you see of each person of the Trinity—the Father, the Son and the Holy Spirit? (Although the Holy Spirit is mentioned by name only in verses 13 and 14, his activity is assumed throughout.)

Verse 3 is the first place Paul uses the remarkable expression "in the heavenly realms," which occurs five times in Ephesians and nowhere else in his letters. "In the heavenly realms" is neither sky nor grace nor glory, nor any literal spatial abode, but rather the unseen world of spiritual reality. The five uses of the expression in Ephesians indicate that this is the sphere in which the "rulers and authorities" continue to operate (3:10; 6:12), in which Christ reigns supreme and his people reign with him (1:20; 2:6), and in which therefore God blesses us with every spiritual blessing in Christ (1:3).

---

4. How do these blessings relate to the past (v. 4), the present (v. 7) and the future (v. 10)?

Mark well the statement: *he chose us in him.* The juxtaposition of the three pronouns is emphatic. God put us and Christ together in his mind. He determined to make us (who did not yet exist) his own children through the redeeming work of Christ (which had not yet taken place). It was a definite decision. It also arose from his entirely unmerited favor. When he chose us, we were unholy and blameworthy, and therefore deserving not of adoption but of judgment. Further, he made us his children.

5. How are you affected by the fact that God had a plan for you before the world was created?

6. What is this purpose of God for the future (v. 10)?

7. What do you think it will mean to have all things under the head of Christ?

Summary: At this point it may be wise to pause a moment and consider how much all of us need to develop Paul's broad perspective. Paul was a prisoner in Rome. Not indeed in a cell or dungeon, but still under house arrest and handcuffed to a Roman soldier. Though his wrist was chained and his body was confined, his heart and mind inhabited eternity. He peered back "before the creation of the world" (v. 4) and on to the fullness of time (v. 10), and grasped hold of what "we have" now (v. 7) and ought to be now (v. 4) in the light of those two eternities.

How blinded is our vision in comparison with Paul's! Easily and naturally we slip into a preoccupation with our own petty little affairs. But we need to see time in the light of eternity and our present privileges and obligations in the light of our past election and future perfection. Then, if we shared the apostle's perspective, we would also share his praise. For doctrine leads to doxology as well as to duty. Life would become worship, and we would bless God constantly for having blessed us so richly in Christ

---

8. *Read Ephesians 1:11-14.* In these verses it seems that Paul is alluding to the church as God's "inheritance" and "possession." These words used to be applied exclusively to the one nation of Israel but are now reapplied to an international people whose common factor is that they are all "in Christ." The fact that the same vocabulary is used of both peoples indicates the spiritual continuity between them. How did we become God's possession (vv. 5, 9, 11-12)?

How does it feel to think of yourself as God's inheritance and possession?

---

9. Describe the Holy Spirit and his role in fulfilling this purpose of God (vv. 13-14).

---

10. Notice the repeated phrase, "to the praise of his glory" in verses 5-6, 12, 14. What does this tell you about why God created us?

---

11. What does it mean to live "to the praise of his glory"?

Apply

■ Everything that we have and are in Christ both comes from God and returns to God. It begins in his will and ends in his glory. Yet such Christian talk comes into violent collision with the human-centeredness and self-centeredness of the world. Fallen humanity, imprisoned in its own little ego, has an almost boundless confidence in the power of its own will and an almost insatiable appetite for the praise of its own glory. But the people of God have at least begun to be turned inside out. The new society has new values and new ideals. For God's people are God's possession who live by God's will and for God's glory.

How is your life affected by all the spiritual blessings you have received in Christ Jesus?

_____

How does your life need to change so that you are living to the praise of God's glory?

_____

How can you influence your Christian community to live for God's glory?

Pray ──

■ In silence reflect on all that we have in Christ Jesus. Praise God for each and all of the spiritual blessings he has given to you, past, present and future. Ask the Holy Spirit to make them a reality in your life.

2
A LIFE OF PRAYER

Ephesians 1:15-23

*S*o often we as individuals and we the church forget the supply line of our life. In fact we are guilty of attempting to provide the power to live this Christian life from within ourselves. Not so with Paul.

Paul's life and ministry were saturated in prayer. In fact all of Ephesians 1 is prayer. Paul is addressing God while thinking about the Ephesians. We have already looked at the great benediction in which he blesses God for having blessed us in Christ. Now we will consider the intercession that Paul makes for the Ephesians. It is vital that we not only maintain a high level of prayer in order to enjoy a healthy Christian life, but that we also preserve a balance of praise and prayer—as Paul models.

Open

■ In what ways do you struggle to maintain a consistent life of prayer and praise?

Study

1. *Read Ephesians 1:15-23.* How would you describe the tone of these verses?

---

2. What motivates Paul to pray for the Ephesians?

---

3. List the requests that he makes for them in this prayer.

Despite his unceasing gratitude to God for the Ephesians, Paul still is not satisfied with them. So what is his request? It is not that they may receive a "second blessing" but rather that they may appreciate to the fullest possible extent the implications of the blessings they have already received. So the essence of his prayer for them is "that you may know" (v. 18).

We must not overlook this emphasis. Growth in knowledge is indispensable to growth in holiness. The "knowledge" for which Paul prays adds the knowledge of experience to the knowledge of understanding. More than this, it emphasizes "that you may know him better" (v. 17), that is, come to know truths about him. There is no higher knowledge than the knowledge of God himself.

---

4. Why would the "Spirit of wisdom and revelation" (v. 17) help the Ephesians to know God better?

---

5. What does it mean to "know" God?

6. In biblical usage the heart is the whole inward self, comprising mind as well as emotion. What do you think it means to have "the eyes of your heart . . . enlightened" (v. 18)?

7. The call of God takes us back to the very beginning of our Christian lives. "Those he predestined, he also called; those he called, he also justified" (Romans 8:30). Think about what it is to be called by God. Why is this a source of hope for us?

8. God's inheritance points to the end of our lives, to that final inheritance of which the Holy Spirit is the guarantee (v. 14). Based on what you know from the New Testament, describe this glorious inheritance.

9. Describe God's incomparably great power according to verses 19-22.

10. Why is the resurrection and ascension such a vivid demonstration of divine power?

11. What would it look like to see that power at work in the church today?

Summary: The thrust of Paul's prayer is that his readers may have a thorough knowledge of God's call, inheritance and power, especially the latter. But how do Christians grow in understanding? Some will reply that knowledge depends on the enlightenment of the Holy Spirit. And they are right, at least in part. For Paul prays that "the Spirit of wisdom and revelation" may increase their knowledge of God and enlighten the eyes of their hearts. We have no liberty to infer from this, however, that our responsibility is solely to pray and to wait for illumination, and not at all to think. Others make the opposite mistake: they use their minds and think but leave little room for the enlightenment of the Holy Spirit.

The apostle Paul brings the two together. First he prays that the eyes of his readers' hearts may be enlightened to know God's power. Then he teaches that God has already supplied historical evidence of his power by raising and exalting Jesus. It is precisely as we use our minds to ponder what God has done in Christ that the Spirit will open our eyes to grasp its implications.

Apply —————————————————————
■ In what ways would you like to know God better?

What difference would it make in your life if your eyes were more opened to the hope of God's call?

The church is central to God's plan (vv. 22-23). What role does the church play in your life?

Pray—————————————————————
■ Pray the content of this prayer for your church, yourself and one other Christian friend.

3
A LIFE OF RESURRECTION

Ephesians 2:1-10

*H*ave good and thoughtful people ever been more depressed about the human predicament than they are today? Of course, every age is bound to have a blurred vision of its own problems, because it is too close to them to get them into focus. And every generation breeds new prophets of doom. Nevertheless, the media enables us to grasp the worldwide extent of evil, and it makes the current scene look dark.

Against the sober background of our world, Ephesians 2 stands out in striking relevance. Paul first plumbs the depths of pessimism about humankind and then rises to the heights of optimism about God. Paul paints a vivid contrast between what humankind is by nature and what it can become by grace.

Open
■ What do you think life would be like for you right now if you had not become a Christian?

Study
■ *Read Ephesians 2:1-3.* It is important to set this paragraph in its context. We

have been considering Paul's prayer (1:15-23) that his readers' inward eyes might be enlightened by the Holy Spirit to know the implications of God's call to them, the wealth of his inheritance which awaits them in heaven and above all the surpassing greatness of his power which is available for them meanwhile. Of this power God has given a supreme historical demonstration by raising Christ from the dead and exalting him over all the powers of evil. But he has given a further demonstration of it by raising and exalting us with Christ, and so delivering us from the bondage of death and evil. This paragraph, then, is really a part of Paul's prayer that they (and we) might know how powerful God is. Its first few words emphasize this: "And you being dead."

---

1. What were the Ephesians like before they met Christ?

The biblical statement about the "deadness" of non-Christians may not seem to square with the facts. Lots of people who make no Christian profession whatever, who even openly repudiate Jesus Christ, appear to be very much alive. One has the vigorous body of an athlete, another the lively mind of a scholar, a third the vivacious personality of a filmstar. Are we to say that such people, if Christ has not saved them, are dead? Yes, for in the sphere which matters supremely (which is neither the body, nor the mind, nor the personality, but the soul), they have no life. And you can tell it.

---

2. What symptoms of being "dead in transgressions and sins" do you see in those you know who are not Christians?

---

3. Before Jesus Christ set us free, we were subject to oppressive influences from both within and without. To what forces are non-Christians enslaved (vv. 2-3)?

4. How have you seen these forces at work?

We cannot shift all the blame for our slavery to sin on to "the world, the flesh and the devil" and accept no responsibility for it. On the contrary, it is significant that in these verses "you" and "we" are not identified with these forces but distinguished from them, although enslaved by them. We are called "God's rebel subjects" (v. 2 NEB). We had rebelled, knowingly and voluntarily, against the loving authority of God and so had fallen under the dominion of Satan.

---

5. What does it mean to be objects of God's wrath?

Summary: Paul is not giving us a portrait of some particularly decadent tribe or degraded segment of society, or even of the extremely corrupt paganism of his own day. No, this is the biblical diagnosis of fallen humanity in fallen society everywhere. True, Paul begins with an emphatic *you*, indicating in the first place his Gentile readers in Asia Minor, but he quickly goes on to write (v. 3) that "all of us also lived" in the same way (thus adding himself and his fellow Jews), and he concludes verse 3 with a reference to "the rest" of humankind. This then is the apostle's estimate of everyone without God, of the universal human condition.

---

6. *Read Ephesians 2:4-10.* In contrast to the desperate fallen condition of human beings, what three things has God done for us?

Paul coins three verbs, which take up what God did in Christ and links us to Christ in these events. These verbs ("made alive, "raised" and "seated us") refer to the three successive historical events in the saving career of Jesus. These are normally called the resurrection, the ascension and the session. We declare our belief in them when we say the Apostles' Creed: "The third day he rose again from the dead, he ascended into heaven, and he sits at the right hand of God the Father." Paul is affirming that God not only quickened, raised and seated Christ—but also us with him.

---

7. What do we learn about God's desires for us from these verses?

---

8. What does it mean to be "made alive with Christ" (v. 5)?

---

9. What are the implications of being "raised up with Christ," of being seated with him "in the heavenly realms"?

---

10. Why does Paul work so hard to make it crystal clear that this salvation is by grace, not our works or human effort?

---

11. How does Paul move our salvation from "it" to being intimately personal in verse 10?

---

12. Based on what you have seen in this passage, how would you explain what salvation is?

Summary: This passage begins with *"But . . . God."* These two monosyllables set against the desperate condition of fallen humankind the gracious initiative and sovereign action of God. We were the objects of his wrath, *but God* out of the great love with which he loved us had mercy on us. We were dead, and the dead do not rise, *but God* made us alive with Christ. We were slaves, in a situation of dishonor and powerlessness, *but God* has raised us with Christ and set us at his own right hand, in a position of honor and power. Thus God has taken action to reverse our condition in sin. It is essential to hold both parts of this contrast together, namely, what we are by nature and what we are by grace.

Apply ————————————————————————

■ Christians are sometimes criticized for being morbidly preoccupied with their sin and guilt. The criticism is not fair when we are facing the facts about ourselves (for it is never unhealthy to look reality in the face), but only when we fail to go on to glory in God's mercy and grace. How do you respond to God's marvelous grace as you see it described here and experience it in your life?

How does this passage help you to point others away from yourself and toward God?

What hinders you from doing the good works God prepared for you to do?

Pray ————————————————————————

■ Spend a few moments reflecting on your spiritual condition before you met Christ. Now praise him for the work of grace that he has done in you.

4
A NEW HUMANITY

Ephesians 2:11-22

*H*ostility between human beings is not an invention of the twentieth century. It has run rampant since the fall of humanity, when we chose to be hostile to God. Alienation between individuals, nations, races, and even hostility between Christians is no stranger to us. The Bible speaks of human alienation—alienation from God our Creator and alienation from each other. Nothing is more dehumanizing than this breakdown of human relationships. We are strangers in a world where we should feel at home, aliens instead of citizens.

Open

■ As you think about your world, what examples of hostility between groups of people come to mind?

Study

1. *Read Ephesians 2:11-13.* Trace the spiritual biography of the Gentiles in this passage.

2. The Jews had an immense contempt for the Gentiles. The Gentiles, said the Jews, were created by God to be fuel for the fires of hell. God, they said, loves only Israel, of all the nations that he had made. What do you think it would be like to be a Gentile in this pre-Christian condition?

3. What did Jesus do for the Gentiles?

The parallel between the two halves of Ephesians 2 is obvious. First comes in both cases a description of life without Christ: "dead" (vv. 1-3) and "excluded" (vv. 11-12). Then follows, again in both cases, the great "But . . . God" (v. 4) and "But now" (v. 13). The main distinction is that in the second half Paul is stressing the Gentile experience.

4. What individual Christians or groups of Christians are you separated from (because of theological, cultural, denominational, racial or economic differences)?

5. *Read Ephesians 2:14-18.* How did Jesus bring the Jews and Gentiles together?

How can the apostle say that Christ abolished the law when Christ himself declared the opposite, that he had not come to abolish it but to fulfill it? The context of the Sermon on the Mount shows that Jesus was referring to the *moral* law. He was teaching the difference between Pharisaic righteousness and Christian righteousness, and urging that Christian righteousness involves a deep and radical obedience to the law. Paul's primary reference here, however, seems to be to the ceremonial law and "its rules and regulations" (NEB), that is, to circumcision (the main physical distinction between Jews and Gentiles, v. 11), material sacrifices, dietary regulations and rules about ritual "cleanness" and "uncleanness" which governed social relationships.

6. What is the significance of the fact that Jesus "preached peace to you who were far away and peace to those who were near" (v. 17)?

7. What does it mean to have access to the Father through one Spirit (v. 18)?

8. The status of the Gentles has dramatically changed. Instead of being refugees they now have a home. *Read Ephesians 2:19-22.* What is the final outcome of Christ's destroying the wall of hostility (vv. 19-22)?

9. Think about this spiritual building that is being constructed. How are the apostles and prophets the foundation?

10. Why is Jesus considered the chief cornerstone of this building?

11. How do you respond to being a part of God's new society, built together into a holy temple in which God lives?

Summary: It would be hard to exaggerate the grandeur of this vision of the new society that God has brought into being. But when we turn from the ideal portrayed in Scripture to the concrete realities experienced in the church today, it is very different and a very tragic story. For even in the church there is often alienation, disunity and discord. Now Christians erect new barriers in place of the old which Christ has demolished: now racism; now personal animosities engineered by pride, prejudice, jealousy and the unforgiving spirit; now a divisive system of caste or class; now a separation of clergy from laity, as if they were separate breeds of human being; and now a denominationalism which turns churches into sect and contradicts the unity of Christ's church.

Apply

■ How does this passage encourage you about your relationship with God?

with other believers?

How do you take for granted being near to God?

What role do you think you might have in breaking down barriers between yourself and others?

Pray

■ Praise God for bringing you so close to himself and to other believers when at one time you were so far away. Ask him to work in you his grace to live out the truth that the dividing wall of hostility is down between all believers.

5
A NEW MINISTRY

Ephesians 3:1-13

Anyone who is acquainted with Paul knows how seriously he took his call from God to be an apostle. The book of Ephesians is no exception. After two chapters of explanation about what Christ has done, first for all of humanity and then specifically for the Gentiles, Paul switches the topic to himself and his unique ministry to the Gentiles.

Today God continues to call believers first to himself and then to his purpose for their lives. God's purpose for us might resemble the kind of unique ministry that Paul had. It might not. But he does call. And he wants us to respond to that call with the same faithfulness Paul did.

Open

■ Describe a situation in which you felt called to do something.

Study

1. *Read Ephesians 3:1-13.* What do you learn about Paul in this passage?

2. Why would Paul consider himself a prisoner of Christ when in reality he was a prisoner of Nero?

3. This chapter opens with the words "For this reason," connecting this chapter to chapter 2. Why, based on what he had just said, do you think he was a prisoner for the sake of the Gentiles?

4. Twice Paul uses the expression "God's grace [that was] given [to] me" (vv. 2, 7). What two privileges had God in unmerited favor given him (vv. 3, 7-8)?

5. What was this mystery which was made known to Paul through special revelation (v. 6)?

We need to realize that the word *mystery* is different in Greek than in English. In Greek, although it means a "secret" as in English, it is no longer closely guarded but open. Christian "mysteries" are truths which, although beyond human discovery, have been revealed by God and so now belong openly to the whole church.

6. In verse 8 how does Paul describe himself?

7. In what ways are you encouraged in the ways you serve God by this description of Paul?

8. What is Paul's attitude toward his ministry to the Gentiles? Give examples for your answer.

The statements in verses 5 and 9 that the mystery was not made known in other generations have puzzled Bible readers because the Old Testament did reveal that God had a purpose for the Gentiles. It promised, for example, that all the families of the earth would be blessed through Abraham's posterity; that the Messiah would receive the nations as its inheritance; that Israel would be given as a light to the nations; and that one day the nations would make a pilgrimage to Jerusalem and even "flow to it" like a mighty river. But what was not revealed was the radical nature of God's plan which was that the theocracy (the Jewish nation under God's rule) would be terminated and replaced by a new international community, the church; that this church would be "the body of Christ," organically united to him; and that Jews and Gentiles would be incorporated into Christ and his church on equal terms, without any distinction.

9. In contrast to keeping this mystery hidden in the past, what is God's intent now for his church (vv. 10-11)?

10. Why do you think God would want his wisdom made known to the rulers and authorities in the heavenly realms?

11. What is Paul's attitude and teaching about the church of Jesus Christ?

Summary: The major lesson taught by this first half of Ephesians 3 is the centrality of the church. Some people construct a Christianity which consists entirely of a personal relationship to Jesus Christ and has virtually nothing to do with the church. Others make a grudging concession to the need for church membership, but add that they have given up the ecclesiastical institution as hopeless. Every church in every place at every time is in need of reform and renewal. But we need to beware lest we despise the church of God and are blind to his work in history.

Apply
■ How do you respond to the idea of taking the message of Jesus Christ to those in your world who need it?

How do you see God's grace in your daily life and ministry?

What is your attitude toward the church of Jesus Christ, and how might your attitude need to change?

Pray
■ Ask God to open your eyes to his grace in your life. Ask him to make clear to you his call to serve. Praise God for his church, the body of Christ. Ask him to help you to grow in your and appreciation of the church.

6
A NEW CONFIDENCE

Ephesians 3:14-21

*O*ne of the best ways to discover a Christian's chief anxieties and ambitions is to study the content of their prayers and the intensity with which they pray them. We all pray about what concerns us and are evidently not concerned about matters we do not include in our prayers. Prayer expresses desire. For example, when Paul prayed for the salvation of his Israelite kinsfolk, he wrote of his "heart's desire and prayer to God for them."

As the hymn puts it, "Prayer is the soul's sincere desire, unuttered or expressed." This is certainly true of this second prayer of Paul's in Ephesians. He pours out his heart to God.

Open
■ What have you learned from a Christian whose background is different from yours? (Consider those who are different in terms of age, denomination, ethnicity, gender, social status and so on.)

Study

1. *Read Ephesians 3:14-19.* List all the requests in this prayer.

What repeated themes stand out in these requests?

2. Again Paul begins the passage, "For this reason." What was the reason for Paul's prayer?

We see an important principle of prayer here. The basis of Paul's prayer was his knowledge of God's purpose. It was because of what God had done in Christ and revealed to Paul that he had the necessary warrant to pray. For the indispensable prelude to all petition is the revelation of God's will. We have no authority to pray for anything which God has not revealed to be his will. This is why Bible reading and prayer should always go together. For it is in Scripture that God has disclosed his will, and it is in prayer that we ask him to do it.

3. How is God characterized in verses 14 and 15?

4. How does our understanding of God impact how we approach him in prayer?

5. Why would Paul ask that Christ might dwell in their hearts when he is praying for Christians (v. 17)?

6. As you think about all that has been explained in the book of Ephesians so far, why is love such an important element of Paul's prayer?

7. We shall have power to comprehend these dimensions of Christ's love, Paul adds, only *with all the saints* (v. 18). Why is this emphasized? (Is it possible to know Jesus apart from other Christians?)

8. What effect would it have on the church if the prayer that we all could grasp the love of Christ were answered?

Although we may grasp dimensions of Christ's love to some extent with our minds, we cannot "know" it in our experience. It is too broad, long, deep and high even for all the saints together to grasp. It *surpasses knowledge.*

Paul has already used this "surpassing" word of God's grace; now he uses it of his love. Christ's love is as unknowable as his riches are unsearchable (v. 8). Doubtless we shall spend eternity exploring his inexhaustible riches of grace and love.

9. How have you seen this prayer answered in your church?

10. *Read Ephesians 3:20-21.* How is God's power demonstrated by Paul's great benediction in verses 20-21?

---

11. How accurately does the benediction in verses 20-21 communicate your perception and expectation of God? Explain.

---

12. How is this whole prayer evidence of the freedom and confidence with which we can approach God?

---

13. How does this prayer demonstrate the centrality of the church in God's plan for the world?

Summary: Paul's prayer relates to the fulfillment of his vision for God's new society of love. He asks that its members may be strengthened to love and to know the love of Christ, though this surpasses knowledge. But then he turns from the love of God past knowing to the power of God past imagining, from limitless love to limitless power. For he is convinced, as we must be, that only divine power can generate divine love in the divine society.

To add anything more would be inappropriate, except the doxology. "To him be glory," Paul exclaims, to this God of resurrection power, who alone can make the dream come true. The power comes from him; the glory must go to him. To him be glory in the church and in Christ Jesus together, in the body and in the Head, in the bride and in the Bridegroom, in the community of peace and in the Peacemaker, to all generations (in history) for ever and ever (in eternity), Amen.

Apply
■ How freely and confidently do you approach God?

It takes the whole people of God to understand the whole love of God, *all the saints* together—Jews and Gentiles, men and women, young and old, black and white—with all their varied backgrounds and experiences. In what current situation or relationship do you have the opportunity to learn from another Christian?

How would you like to grow in the way that you pray for your church?

Pray
■ Kneel quietly and in worship before the Father, from whom his whole family in heaven and earth derives its name. Pray Paul's prayer for your church.

7
UNITY

Ephesians 4:1-16

*S*ooner or later, and sooner is better, we have to move from studying the content of the gospel to living out the gospel in our everyday lives. At this point in Ephesians Paul moves from the explanation of God's new society to its standards. He turns from exposition to exhortation, from what God has done to what we must be and do, from mind-stretching theology to its down-to-earth, concrete implications in everyday living. The first standard that he emphasizes is unity.

Open

■ How do you think that unity is different from uniformity?

Study

■ Instruction, intercession and exhortation constitute a formidable trio of weapons in any Christian teacher's armory. Paul has taught the Ephesians, and he has prayed for them, now he addresses to them a solemn appeal. *Read Ephesians 4:1-6.*

1. What does Paul beg the Ephesians to do?

2. Because God's people are called to be one people, they must manifest their unity. Define each of the characteristics (humbleness, gentleness, patience, forbearance, love) to which Paul calls them in verse 2.

The people we immediately like are the people who give us the respect we consider we deserve, while the people we immediately, instinctively dislike are those who treat us like dirt. In other words personal vanity is a key factor in all our relationships. If, however, instead of maneuvering for the respect of others (which is pride) we give them our respect by recognizing their God-given worth (which is humility), we shall be promoting harmony in God's new society.

---

3. How would following the instructions in verse 2 contribute to the unity of the church?

---

4. In what kinds of situations do you find that you struggle with the tension between humility and pride?

---

5. In verses 4-6 Paul repeats the word *one* seven times and three of those allude to the persons of the Trinity. How does unity of our God relate to Christian unity?

---

6. The apostle tells us to "make every effort to keep the unity of the Spirit" (v. 3). We are to "spare no effort" (NEB), and in Greek it is a call for continuous, diligent activity. Why would Paul need to urge the Ephesian believers to make every effort to keep the unity just before making such a strong statement about the body being one in verse 4?

7. *Read Ephesians 4:7-16.* How does Paul make it clear that unity does not mean uniformity?

8. What do we learn about the giver of spiritual gifts in verses 9-10?

9. What do we learn about the purpose of spiritual gifts (vv. 12-16)?

10. What does Paul mean by building up the body of Christ, according to verses 13-16?

11. The church grows by truth and love. What are the extremes of how this happens in some of our churches?

Summary: Here then is Paul's vision for the church. God's society is to display charity, unity, diversity and growing maturity. These are the characteristics of a life worthy of God, which the apostle begs us to lead.

The more we share Paul's perspective, the deeper will be our discontent with the ecclesiastical status quo. Some of us are too conservative, too complacent, too ready to acquiesce in the present situation and to resist change. Others are too radical, wanting to dispense with the institution altogether. Instead we need to grasp more clearly the kind of new society God wants his church to be. Then we shall not be content either with things as they are or with partial solutions, but rather will pray and work for the church's total renewal.

Complacency is unworthy of the church's calling. In contrast to it the apostle sets before us the picture of a deepening fellowship, an eagerness to maintain visible Christian unity (and to recover it if it is lost), an active every-member ministry, and a steady growth into maturity by holding the truth in love. We need to keep this biblical ideal clearly before us. Only then shall we live a life that is worthy of it.

Apply ————————————————————————

■ Which of the qualities of unity discussed in this passage have helped you experience unity with others?

————————————————————————

What do you to do to maintain and work for the unity of the Spirit in your Christian community?

————————————————————————

How would you like to grow in the ways you use your spiritual gifts to fulfill the purposes listed in verses 11-13? (This could include thinking of ways to become more familiar with your gifts.)

————————————————————————

Pray ————————————————————————

■ Thank God for the marvelous unity that he has made available to us in the church. Confess to him the ways that you have failed to strive to maintain the unity in your church. Ask him to change you and build into you the five foundation stones of Christian unity.

8
PURITY

Ephesians 4:17—5:4

*S*ome churches in the name of unity allow their members to believe
whatever they wish to believe and behave in whatever way they want to
behave—to make sure everyone is happy and all *stay together*. On the other
hand are those who in the name of purity criticize and scrutinize others
who truly love and follow Jesus. Instead of separation from the world, they
separate themselves from brothers and sisters

Paul is not only concerned about the unity of the church but her purity.
This section of Ephesians is Paul's perspective on purity.

Open

■ On a scale from 1-10, 10 being most pure, how would you describe the
purity of the church today? Explain.

Study

■ In this section Paul gives specific instruction about actively cultivating
purity in the Christian life. Holiness is not a condition that we drift into. We
are not passive spectators of a sanctification God works in us. On the

contrary, we have purposefully to "put off" from us all conduct that is incompatible with our new life in Christ, and to "put on" a lifestyle compatible with it. *Read Ephesians 4:17-24.*

---

1. Paul insists that the Ephesian Christians must no longer live like pagans (Gentiles). How are the pagans described?

---

2. Look carefully at this description. Explain the logical steps of their downward path of evil.

---

3. From verses 20-24 describe the process of moral education that the Christians experienced.

Christ is himself the substance of Christian teaching. When Jesus Christ is at once the subject and the object and the environment of the moral instruction being given, we may have confidence that it is truly Christian. For *truth is in Jesus.*

But what sort of Christ do they learn? Not just the Word made flesh, the unique God-man, who died, rose and reigns. More than that. The context implies that we must also preach Christ's lordship, the rule of righteousness he ushered in and all the moral demands of the new life. The Christ whom the Ephesians had learned was calling them to standards and values totally at variance with their former pagan life.

---

4. What is the role of the mind in the behavior of both the pagans (v. 18) and the believers (vv. 20-24)?

5. What then is the significance of truth and ignorance in living a life of purity?

6. What are you doing to renew your mind in Christ?

Read Ephesians 4:29—5:4. At their conversion the Ephesians put off their old humanity (like a rotten garment) and put on (like clean clothing) the new humanity, recreated in God's image. It is because of this that they could logically be commanded to put away all the practices which belong to that old and rejected life. Their new behavior must be completely consistent with the kind of persons they have become.

It is marvelous to see how easily Paul can descend from lofty theological talk about our two humanities, about the Christ we have learned and the new creation we have experienced, to the nitty-gritty of Christian behavior.

7. List each of the six examples of sin that we are to put off, noting the positive command with each instruction.

Verses	Sin to Put Off	Positive Command
4:25		
4:26-27		implied: make amends
4:28		
4:29-30		
4:31—5:2		
5:3-4		

8. What do all of these have in common?

---

9. What reason is given or implied in each case for the commands?

---

10. Why do you think Paul introduces the Holy Spirit in 4:30?

---

11. In 4:25 Paul states, "For we are all members of one body." What would be the affects of obeying these commands upon the body of Christ?

Summary: This passage is a stirring summons to the unity and purity of the church, but it is more than that. It is the integration of Christian experience (what we are), Christian theology (what we believe) and Christian ethics (how we behave). It emphasizes that being, thought and action belong together and must never be separated. For what we are governs how we think, and how we think determines how we act. We are God's new society, a people who have put off the old life and put on the new; that is what he has made us. So we need to recall this by daily renewing of our minds, remembering how we learned the truth in Jesus and thinking Christianly about ourselves and our new status.

Apply
■ To which of these areas of sin that we are to put off are you most vulnerable?

How does who you are in Christ affect the way you want to live?

Holiness is not a mystical condition experienced in relation to God, in isolation from human beings. You cannot be good in a vacuum but only in the real world of people. How can others help you to become more pure?

Pray
■ Thank God for his call to a life of holiness. Ask him to reveal to you sin that needs to be put off and the good garments that he wants you to put on. Thank him for the work of the Holy Spirit in your life.

9
RIGHTEOUSNESS

Ephesians 5:5-21

*L*et no one say that doctrine does not matter! Good conduct arises out of good doctrine. It is only when we have grasped clearly who we are in Christ that the desire will grow within us to live a life that is worthy of our calling and fitting to our character as God's new society. We must grasp who we are and experience radical change in order to live as children of light in the fullness of the Holy Spirit. In this section of scripture Paul moves on from models of Christian behavior to motivation, adding powerful incentives to righteous living.

Open

■ What is it like for you to know something for sure?

Study

1. *Read Ephesians 5:5-7.* What warning does Paul give in verses 5-7?

We must be cautious in our application of this severe statement. It should not be understood as teaching that a single immoral thought, word or deed is enough to disqualify us from heaven; otherwise, which of us would ever qualify for admission? For those who fall into such sins through weakness, but afterwards repent in shame and humility, there is forgiveness. The immoral person described here is one who has turned to this way of life without shame or penitence.

2. In this context what would it mean to be deceived with empty words?

3. Why would Paul call immoral, impure or greedy people idolaters?

4. In what areas of your life are you most tempted toward idolatry?

5. *Read Ephesians 5:8-21.* Paul contrasts light with darkness to say more about holy living. As light in the Lord, how are we to live (vv. 8-21)?

6. Why is it important that sin is made visible (v. 13)?

7. Anything that becomes visible is light. How can Christians transform darkness into light?

8. Note that Paul says, "Be very careful" (v. 15). We all take care over the things which seem to us to matter—our job, our education, our home and family, our hobbies, our appearance. So as Christians we must be watchful over our Christian life. How can we take care of our Christian life?

---

9. What are the characteristics of a wise person according to verses 15-17?

---

10. Why is it important to make the most of every opportunity?

---

11. How would making the most of every opportunity combat the evil days? If you're doing good, you're not doing bad. You're encouraging others to do good. You're discouraging

---

12. What are the beneficial results of being filled with the Holy Spirit (vv. 19-21)? them from doing bad.

Although the text reads that we are to give thanks *always* and *for everything*, we must not press those words literally. For we cannot thank God for blatant evil. God's children learn not to argue with him in their suffering but to trust him, and indeed to thank him for his loving providence by which he can turn even evil to good purposes. But that is praising God for being God; it is not praising him for evil. To do this would be to react insensitively to people's pain (when Scripture tells us to weep with those who weep) and to condone and even encourage evil (when Scripture tells us to hate and to resist the devil). So then the "everything" for which we are to give thanks to God must be qualified by its content, namely, *to God the Father, . . . in the name of our Lord Jesus Christ.*

---

13. Why do you think it would be necessary to be filled with the Holy Spirit in order to submit to one another?

Summary: All the wholesome results of the fullness of the Holy Spirit concern our relationships. If we are filled with the Spirit, we shall be harmoniously related both to God (worshipping him with joy and thanksgiving) and to each other (speaking and submitting to one another). In brief, Spirit-filled believers love God and love each other, which is hardly surprising since the first fruit of the Spirit is love.

Apply

■ The light metaphor speaks vividly of Christian openness and transparency, of living joyfully in the presence of Christ, with nothing to hide or fear. As a child of light how do you expose evil around you?

How could you live more wisely?

Pray

■ Recommit yourself to God as a child of light. Tell him of your desire to live as such in a dark world and to please him. Ask him to reveal to you sin and idolatry that separate you from him.

10
LOVE

Ephesians 5:21-33

What is the point of peace in the church if there is no peace in the home? The divine family ceases to be a credible concept if it is not itself subdivided into human families which display God's love. Sadly, few Christians know how high and mysterious is the call of God to marriage! In a culture which screams "do whatever feels good" and "me first," it is especially difficult, even as followers of Jesus, to give our marriage the time and energy which it deserves—or even the commitment it takes to make it last. As in all other aspects of the Christian life, the community, the new creation of God, is vital in marriage.

In this section of Ephesians Paul marvelously combines doctrine with practical instruction about marriage, as he enters into the topic of new relationships in this new society of God. If our Christian faith is of any practical value, it must teach us how to behave Christianly at home.

Open ─────────────────────────────

■ Whether you are married or single, when is it hard for you to humbly submit your will to that of another person?

Study

1. *Read Ephesians 5:21-33.* Throughout the passage, what is said about the church?

---

2. Why is verse 21 an excellent opening statement to this section on marriage?

---

3. What does it mean to submit to the Lord (v. 22)?

---

4. What do we learn from verses 22-24 about how a wife is to regard her husband?

---

5. Why is the wife supposed to submit to her husband?

---

6. How do you react to the notion of submitting to someone else?

We must not interpret what Paul writes about submission in a way which contradicts the fundamental attitudes of Jesus, who treated women with courtesy and honor in an age in which they were despised. Nor in a way which contradicts Paul's teaching on our oneness in Christ. In the light of the teaching of Jesus and Paul, we can confidently affirm the dignity of womanhood, the equality before God of all human beings and the unity of all believers as fellow members of God's family and Christ's body.

It is important to grasp the difference between persons on one hand and roles on the other. Once we see this distinction, then those who hold an office—whether rulers, magistrates, husbands, parents or employers—have a certain God-given authority which they expect others to acknowledge. People have equal dignity as Godlike beings, but different God-appointed roles.

Paul defines the husband's headship in relation to the headship of Christ the redeemer. Now Christ's headship of his church has already been described in 4:15-16. It is from Christ as head that the body derives its health and grows into maturity. His headship expresses care rather than control, responsibility rather than rule. The characteristic of his headship is not so much lordship as saviorhood.

---

7. What instructions are given to the husband (vv. 25-33)?

---

8. How has Christ loved the church?

---

9. In your own words, what is the husband's goal for his wife (vv. 26-27)?

---

10. What is the significance of a husband and wife becoming one flesh (vv. 31-32)?

11. Why do you think it is important for the husband to *love* his wife?

the wife to *respect* her husband?

12. In review, how is Christian marriage compared to Christ's relationship with the church?

13. How do you respond to the fact that the marriage of believers represents to the world Christ's relationship to his church?

Summary: We have seen that the essence of Paul's instruction is "wives submit, husbands love" and that these words are different from one another since they recognize the headship which God has given to the husband. Yet when we try to define the two verbs, it is not easy to distinguish clearly between them. What does it mean to submit? It is to give oneself up to somebody. What does it mean to love? It is to give oneself up for somebody, as Christ gave himself up for the church. Thus *submission* and *love* are two aspects of the very same thing, namely, of that selfless self-giving which is the foundation of an enduring and growing marriage.

Apply ─────────────────────────────
■ What would marriages be like if these instructions were followed?

If you are a wife, how can your submission to your husband be more like your submission to Christ?

_____

If you are a husband, how can you love your wife more like Christ loved the church?

_____

How can the Christian community build and support our marriages?

Pray

■ If you are married, thank God for the gift of your marriage and the privilege of representing to the world Christ's relationship with his bride. If you are not married, pray for marriages in your community, that they will grow and represent Christ well.

11
RESPECT

Ephesians 6:1-9

*R*aising children is the hardest thing I have ever done. It is harder than living the Christian life," stated the mother of two lovely daughters. The girls are now adults, wonderful young women who love the Lord and their parents. They gave their parents no unusual trouble while they were growing up. The mother loved being a mom and would not have given that up for anything in the world. However at that point in her journey, she was willing to own that the task of raising children was a difficult one.

Paul now moves from the reciprocal duties of husbands and wives to those of parents and children. Since he addresses the children as well as their parents, he evidently expects whole families to come together for public worship not only to praise God but also to listen to his Word. That children should have been included in the instructions is an indication that they were following the lead of Jesus, who said, "Let the little children come to me" (Mark 10:14). It was a radical change from the callous cruelty toward children which prevailed in the Roman Empire.

Open
■ What word or phrase would you use to describe your relationship with your parents?

Study

1. *Read Ephesians 6:1-4.* How do you see mutual submission (5:21) continuing to be worked out in this passage?

2. What exhortation does Paul give to children (vv. 1-3)?

Obeying parents is part of the natural law that God has written on all hearts. We experience no sense of surprise, therefore, when Paul includes disobedience to parents as a mark both of a decadent society which God has given up to its own godlessness and of "the last days" which began with the coming of Christ. Probably we should interpret the promises in verse 3 in general rather than individual terms. Then what is promised is not so much long life to each child who obeys his parents, as social stability to any community in which children honor their parents.

3. How does society benefit from children following Paul's instructions?

4. How are parents to raise their children?

5. What are ways that parents exasperate their children?

6. What effects do we usually see in children who are raised according to these instructions?

Read Ephesians 6:5-9. It is immediately remarkable that Paul should address himself to slaves at all. The simple fact that he does so indicates that they are accepted members of the Christian community and that he regards them as responsible people to whom, as much as to their masters, he sends a moral appeal.

7. How are Christian slaves to be different then other slaves? Why?

8. What should be the motivation behind the slaves' response to their masters?

9. In this society of slavery what do Christian masters and slaves have in common?

10. Paul admits no privileged superiority in the masters, as if they could themselves dispense with the very courtesies they expect to be shown. How does the theme "for we are members of his body" run throughout this whole section on new relationships (5:21—6:9)?

Summary: The concept of brotherhood, even with slaves, is one of the major themes of Ephesians. For God's new society is the Father's household, or family, all of whose members are related to one another in Christ as brothers and sisters. Even in the first letter he wrote, he could affirm with confidence that all who are in Christ are the sons and daughters of God, and that "there is neither . . . slave nor free . . . for you are all one in Christ Jesus" (Galatians 3:28). A message which thus united master and slave issued its radical challenge to an institution which separated them as proprietor and property. Thereafter it was only a matter of time before slavery would be abolished.

Apply

■ What are practical ways for you to obey and honor your parents?

If you are a parent, how do you avoid exasperating your children?

What implications does this passage have concerning how employers should relate to employees?

What can we learn about how Christians should regard their work?

Pray

■ Celebrate the body of Christ in which we are all equal. Pray for your brothers and sisters in the Lord for whom you work or who work for you. Ask God to work in your children and to help them to grow in their relationship with him.

12
POWER

Ephesians 6:10-24

Without warning the battle cry is sounded. The enemy is named, and the relentless struggle against evil has begun. Because this is a battle that cannot be seen and its casualties can be explained away, the church has a tendency to ignore it or to fight with its own armor and strategies. It is no wonder we experience defeat. We must arise, put on the full armor of God and be strong in his might. This final section of Ephesians tells us how to do that.

Open ───────────────────────────

■ What comes to your mind when you hear the phrase "spiritual warfare"?

Study ───────────────────────────

1. *Read Ephesians 6:10-17*. A thorough knowledge of the enemy and a healthy respect for his prowess are necessary for victory in war. The "wiles of the devil" take many forms, but he is at his wiliest when he succeeds in persuading people that he does not exist. To deny his reality is to expose ourselves all the more to his subtlety. Look carefully at the description of our enemy in verses 11-12. What do you find out?

2. If we underestimate our spiritual enemy, we will see no need for God's armor and go into battle unarmed. With no weapons but our puny strength, we will be quickly defeated. What exhortations does Paul give in verses 10-11 for preparation for battle?

---

3. Why do you think "standing" is emphasized so much?

---

4. Look closely at the six main pieces of the armor of God. Why is each piece vital for spiritual battle?

Piece of Armor	Role in Spiritual Battle
Belt: Usually made of leather, the soldier's belt gathered the tunic together and held the sword, ensuring that the soldier marched unimpeded.	
Breastplate: Covering the soldier's back and front, the breastplate protected the vital organs.	
Boots: The "half boots" of the Roman soldier were made of leather, left the toes free, had heavy studded soles and were strapped to the ankles. They supported long marches and gave a solid stance, which prevented sliding.	
Shield: The oblong shield covered the whole body and was designed to give protection from fire-tipped darts.	
Helmet: Made of bronze, the helmet had an inside lining of felt, making the weight bearable. A hinged visor added frontal protection. Nothing short of an ax could pierce the helmet.	
Sword: This was the only piece of armor used for attack as well as defense.	

5. What do you think are the "flaming arrows of the evil one" (v. 16)?

6. Which pieces of armor have you used most in fighting your battles?

7. *Read Ephesians 6:18-20.* Equipping ourselves with God's armor is not a mechanical operation; it is an expression of our dependence on God. According to verses 18-20 prayer is to pervade all our spiritual warfare. What instructions are given about prayer?

8. What do you think it means to pray in the Spirit?

9. Why is it difficult to pray the way we are told to pray in this passage?

10. How are the kinds of prayers urged in this passage a continuation of the kind of praying Paul has done throughout the book?

11. *Read Ephesians 6:21-24.* What do Paul's final instructions reveal about his relationship with the Ephesians?

12. Of the four words *peace, love, faith* and *grace* which are included in the apostle's final greeting, the two which stand out as particularly appropriate are grace and peace. He began his letter by wishing his readers "grace and peace to you from God our Father and the Lord Jesus Christ" (1:2); he now ends it with a similar reference to grace and peace. Why does Paul focus on these qualities?

13. Again and again we see Paul's desire that the members of God's new society may live in harmony as brothers and sisters, in his family, at peace and in love with him and each other, recognizing that only by God's grace can this dream come true. How have your goals and desires for your Christian community been influenced by studying Ephesians?

Apply

■ God has given us his armor, but it is our responsibility to put it on and to use it confidently against the powers of evil. What do you need to do in order to put it on?

How do you need to shape your prayer life so that you can engage in the battle through prayer?

Pray

■ Spend time quietly reflecting on the battle and the armor. Ask God to give you wisdom and strength for the battle and to help you to put on the whole armor of God.

Guidelines for Leaders

My grace is sufficient for you. (2 Corinthians 12:9)

If leading a small group is something new for you, don't worry. These sessions are designed to be led easily. Because the Bible study questions flow from observation to interpretation to application, you may feel as if the studies lead themselves.

You don't need to be an expert on the Bible or a trained teacher to lead a small group discussion. As a leader, you can guide group members to discover for themselves what the Bible has to say and to listen for God's guidance. This method of learning will allow group members to remember much more of what is said than a lecture would.

This study guide is flexible. You can use it with a variety of groups—students, professionals, neighborhood or church groups. Each study takes forty-five to sixty minutes in a group setting.

There are some important facts to know about group dynamics and encouraging discussion. The suggestions listed below should equip you to effectively and enjoyably fulfill your role as leader.

Preparing for the Study

1. Ask God to help you understand and apply the passage in your own life. Unless this happens, you will not be prepared to lead others. Pray too for the various members of the group. Ask God to open your hearts to the message of his Word and motivate you to action.

2. Read the introduction to the entire guide to get an overview of the topics that will be explored.

3. As you begin each study, read and reread the assigned Bible passage to familiarize yourself with it.

4. This study guide is based on the New International Version of the Bible. It will help you and the group if you use this translation as the basis for your study and discussion.

5. Carefully work through each question in the study. Spend time in meditation and reflection as you consider how to respond.

6. Write your thoughts and responses in the space provided in the study guide. This will help you to express your understanding of the passage clearly.

7. You may want to get a copy of the Bible Speaks Today commentary by John Stott that supplements the Bible book you are studying. The commentary is divided into short units on each section of Scripture so you can easily read the appropriate material each week. This will help you answer tough questions about the passage and its context.

It may help to have a Bible dictionary handy. Use it to look up any unfamiliar words, names or places. (For additional help on how to study a passage, see *How to Lead a LifeGuide Bible Study* from InterVarsity Press, USA.)

8. Take the "Apply" portion of each study seriously. Consider how you need to apply the Scripture to your life. Remember that the group members will follow your lead in responding to the studies. They will not go any deeper than you do.

Leading the Study

1. Begin the study on time. Open with prayer, asking God to help the group to understand and apply the passage.

2. Be sure that everyone in your group has a study guide. Encourage the group to prepare beforehand for each discussion by reading the introduction to the guide and by working through the questions in each study.

3. At the beginning of your first time together, explain that these studies are meant to be discussions, not lectures. Encourage the members of the group to participate. However, do not put pressure on those who may be hesitant to speak during the first few sessions.

4. Have a group member read aloud the introduction at the beginning of the discussion.

5. Every session begins with an "open" question, which is meant to be asked before the passage is read. These questions are designed to introduce the theme of the study and encourage group members to begin to open up. Encourage as many members as possible to participate, and be ready to get the discussion going with your own response.

These opening questions can reveal where our thoughts or feelings need to be transformed by Scripture. That is why it is especially important not to read the passage before the question is asked. The passage will tend to color the honest reactions people would otherwise give because they are, of course, supposed to think the way the Bible does.

6. Have a group member read aloud the passage to be studied.

7. As you ask the study questions, keep in mind that they are designed to be used just as they are written. You may simply read them aloud. Or you may prefer to express them in your own words.

There may be times when it is appropriate to deviate from the study guide. For example, a question may have already been answered. If so, move on to the next question. Or someone may raise an important question not covered in the guide. Take time to discuss it, but try to keep the group from going off on tangents.

8. Avoid answering your own questions. If necessary repeat or rephrase them until they are clearly understood. Or point the group to the commentary woven into the guide to clarify the context or meaning without answering the question. An eager group quickly becomes passive and silent if members think the leader will do most of the talking.

9. Don't be afraid of silence in response to the discussion questions. People may need time to think about the question before formulating their answers.

10. Don't be content with just one answer. Ask, "What do the rest of you think?" or "Anything else?" until several people have given answers to the question.

11. Acknowledge all contributions. Try to be affirming whenever possible. Never reject an answer. If it is clearly off-base, ask, "Which verse led you to that conclusion?" or again, "What do the rest of you think?"

12. Don't expect every answer to be addressed to you, even though this will probably happen at first. As group members become more at ease, they will begin to truly interact with each other. This is one sign of healthy discussion.

13. Don't be afraid of controversy. It can be very stimulating. If you don't re-solve an issue completely, don't be frustrated. Explain that the group will move on and God may enlighten all of you in later sessions.

14. Periodically summarize what the group has said about the passage. This helps to draw together the various ideas mentioned and gives continuity to the study. But don't preach.

15. Conclude your time together with conversational prayer, adapting the prayer suggestion at the end of the study to your group. Ask for God's help in following through on the commitments you've made.

16. End on time.

Many more suggestions and helps can be found in *How to Lead a LifeGuide Bible Study* and *The Big Book on Small Groups* (both from InterVarsity Press, USA). Reading through one of these books would be worth your time.